T0062029

THE
COMPLETE
BOOK OF
CAT NAMES

(THAT YOUR CAT WON'T
ANSWER TO ANYWAY)

Other Books by Bob Eckstein

Footnotes from the World's Greatest Bookstores
The Illustrated History of the Snowman
The Ultimate Cartoon Book of Book Cartoons
Everyone's A Critic: The Ultimate Cartoon Book
All's Fair In Love & War
The Elements of Stress

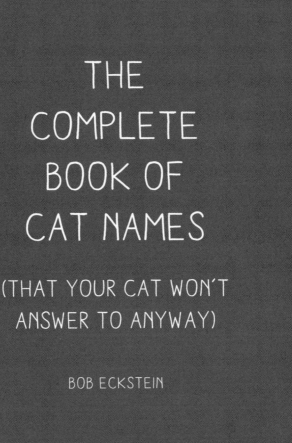

THE
COMPLETE
BOOK OF
CAT NAMES

(THAT YOUR CAT WON'T
ANSWER TO ANYWAY)

BOB ECKSTEIN

Countryman Press

An Imprint of W. W. Norton & Company
Independent Publishers Since 1923

Copyright © 2022 by Bob Eckstein

All rights reserved
Printed in the United States of America

For information about permission to reproduce selections from this book, write to
Permissions, Countryman Press, 500 Fifth Avenue, New York, NY 10110

For information about special discounts for bulk purchases, please contact
W. W. Norton Special Sales at specialsales@wwnorton.com or 800-233-4830

Manufacturing by Versa Press
Book design by Allison Chi
Production manager: Devon Zahn

Countryman Press
www.countrymanpress.com

An imprint of W. W. Norton & Company, Inc.
500 Fifth Avenue, New York, NY 10110
www.wwnorton.com

978-1-68268-703-1

10 9 8 7 6 5 4 3 2 1

"Cats come when they feel like it. Not when they are told."

—*Catwoman* (2004)

CONTENTS

INTRODUCTION

WELCOMING A NEW PET TO YOUR FAMILY IS
a big step for anyone, presenting one of the most challenging questions
in life: what to call it. If you've acquired a kitten or a full-grown cat who
wandered into your life without a name (or with a name you deem inap-
propriate for the feline in front of you), you have a big job ahead of you.
I'm guessing you're aware that many people attempt to name their new
cat with disastrous results?

During the pandemic there was a surge of first-time pet owners, an
unprecedented desire for domestic cats, yet these people had no clue
how to name their new addition, nor did they understand the ramifica-
tions of the task. They heard a name they liked on a TV show or song,
and WHAM!, that became their new pet's name forever. No research,
no deliberation, and no purchasing of this book. Instead there are now
hundreds of cats named Dr. Fauci.

Online studies from respected cat blogs have shown that 80% of cat
owners regret the name they gave their kitten. Number one reason? "It

became too popular." (Number two reason given was, "Too stupid to say in front of company.")

Fear not. Whether you're looking to carry on family tradition or want to try something new and different, *The Complete Book of Cat Names* is packed with witty kitty cat names, making choosing the right one (almost) painless.

This is the perfect book for everyone (except for the approximately one in 30 million people who suffer from *pinaciphobia*, the fear of lists). Because naming your cat is the most important step in your kitten's life (aside from vaccinations and proper name tags), we want to help you decide on the perfect name for your cat. Your kitten's name will set the tone for the rest of his or her personal and possibly professional life, establishing your kitten's online presence with a website, Facebook account, Instagram page, Twitter feed, YouTube, and Pinterest board. That said, it is recommended you read these lists well-rested and sober to get the most out of this book. Never name a kitten while angry or under the influence, but if you insist, we have you covered with a list for that, too.

Feel free to read this book in any order you wish. Truth be told, it was written in no particular order. This book was started over thirty, okay more like forty, years ago in a first-grade classroom at Holy Cross Elementary. Instead of my church studies, I stared out the window at a black cat climbing onto the sill. I remember drawing this creature and naming it. I then came up with other cat drawings and gave those cats names. I drew my classmates and teachers as cats and gave them names. There was Sister Alley Cat, Crystal Rodriguez Cat, and so forth. That summer, bored, I wrote this book, fully aware of my singular talent for naming felines. It was even proofread and illustrated. As an eight-year-old, I had a terrible time landing a literary agent or a publisher for this book and I waited until I was an established writer and the time was right. It was during the pandemic that I dusted off this old book of mine and updated it appropriately, adding over a thousand new names, adding this paragraph to the Introduction, and removing a chapter where over 300 cats were named from the Bible, like Meow Magdalene or any of the CATrinthians. Welcome to a book a half-century in the making.

"Here's what the Art Department came up with."

THE MOST POPULAR CAT NAMES

IF YOU WANT TO CUT TO THE CHASE, LET'S

review today's most popular cat names right up front. You can take one (or perhaps be inspired by another), but is that what you really want? Well, many of you are always on the go and simply don't have time to read an entire book on cat names. You may have already made up your mind that you were not going to delve much deeper. That's fine, not everyone loves books. Or cats. Or is easy to buy a gift for, which may be why you're holding this book in the first place.

If you go with this list, you can't go wrong but at least don't stop at the A's. (Names that were repeated frequently are not included here—your cat deserves better.)

Abby

Agatha

Ali

Alice

Annie

Archie

Athena

Baby

Badger

Bagheera

Basil

Beans

Bear

Belle

Binx

Black-Eyed Pea

Blanche

Blue

Bob

Boo

Boots

Bubbles

Bubi

Buck

Buddy

Calvin

Charlie

Charmin

Chester

Chloe

Cleo

Clyde

Coco

Cooper

Cowboy

Cricket

Daisy

Donut

Dottie

Duchess

Dutch

Effie

Ella

Felix

Fern

Fig

Fluffy

Frank

Frankie

Frannie

Fred

George

Ginger

Griffy

Harley

Harrietta

Hazel

Indy

Ishmael

Ivy

Jack

Jackson

Jasmine

Jax

Joey

Kali

Kiki

Killer

Kitten

Leo	Mr Puss	Smudge
Lily	Mrs Puss	Snowball
Linus	Nala	Sophie
Loki	Nimbus	Sophie II
Lola	Olivia	Spiffy
Louie	Ollie	Spooky
Lucky	Oscar	Stevie
Lucy	Peanut	Sunny
Lucy	Pearl	Sunshine
Lulu	Pee Wee	Sylvester
Maddy	Penny	Tabby
Maggie	Pickle	Tarzan
Maisie	Piper	Tess
Malcolm	Pixie	Theo
Marley	Princess	Thor
Marmalade	Puff	Tiger
Martin	Riley	Tigger
Maurice	Romeo	Tilly
Midnight	Rosie	Tinker Bell
Mila	Ruby	Tizzy
Millie	Sadie	Toby
Milo	Salem	Tucker
Minnie	Sam	Valentino
Miss Kitten	Sam	Walter
Miss Puss	Sasha	Widget
Mister	Scootie	Willow
Mittens	Scout	Willy
Mochi	Shadow	Ziggy
Moose	Sidney	
Morris	Simba	
Mr Cat	Smokey	

ROMAN CAT NAMES

Why would anyone want to give their cat a Roman name? Well, for many, college was their favorite time of life, undoubtedly due to the toga parties, a Roman thing. Others are just still living in the past and want to go way back in time. And then there are those like me, who couldn't get into college or toga parties or into any time machines. We just can't get enough Roman humor and puns.

By the way, yes, Romans had domesticated cats. Of course they did. Actually, Man has tried, and failed, for thousands of years to get cats' attention. David Zax of *Smithsonian* magazine states that domesticated cats date back over 12,000 years to the Near East, just about the time when people began to settle down and farm. *Science* magazine says what transpired was "one of the more successful 'biological experiments' ever undertaken"—cats being used to control mice who were attracted to the harvest and grain. This ancient symbiotic relationship is why we have *Tom & Jerry* cartoons today.

ᛕATLAᛣ!

"Cats rule this town."

Killing a cat in ancient Egypt meant the death penalty, and Egyptians even had cat cemeteries—scientists found 300,000 cat mummies at one! But there is no doubt it was the Romans, inventors of the aqueducts and central sewerage, that made the first kitty litter boxes.

Aristotle	Codex	Maximus Apathy
Attila	Colosseum	Nefertiti
Caser	Delicious Brutus	Sphinx
Chariot	Emperor	Titus
Cicero	Goth	Trojan Cat
Clawdius	Marc Anthony	
Cleocatra	Maximus	

THE MOST POPULAR CAT NAMES IN THE 1800S

Why would anyone name their cat a name from the 1800s? Why are people teaching their cats to skateboard? It's not up to me to judge. These are real names from the 19th century.

Athol	Eulene	Mauline
Balderdash	Everlean	Missouria
Borghild	Furman	Modest
Brunette	Gaynell	Mr. Sunshine
Curly	Gertrude	Norwood
Dagmar	Hertha	Ogden
Dashiell	Hortense	Pinkey
Dimple	Jolly	Ragnhild
Drescell	Keepers, Esq.	Virtue
Edwardine	Letcher	Walburga
Elfrieda	Lurline	Watts

MEDIEVAL CAT NAMES

Are you the type of person who counts the days to the next Renaissance Festival? Can't wait to strap into a constraining low-cut corset so you can show off while eating a ridiculously large turkey leg in public? Do you think it would be funny to address your cat as My Lady? This list is for you.

It should also be mentioned that this was NOT the best time for our beloved favorite pets. Cats were associated with the devil, witches, and evil, which resulted in people killing cats. With fewer cats, there were more rats, making the black plague, which was transmitted by rats, more prevalent.

Antiquity

The Bishop

Black Knight

Box-keeper

Bridge-keeper

Brussels

Camelot

Castle

Charlemagne

Chaucer

Columbus

Crusades

Dragon

Erasmus

Erik the Red

Excalibur

Feudal

Flying Buttress

Friar Tuck

Galahad

Genghis

Goblet

Grail

Green Knight

Guillotine

Gutenberg

Impaler

Jester

Joan of Arc

King

King Arthur

King Henry

Knight

Knight of Ni

Lion-Heart

Lord

Lord Farquaad

Lord of the Floor

Maiden

Marco Polo

Monk

Ogre

Patsy

Peter the Hermit

Pillage

Pinocchio

Pope

Prince Herbert

Prince Meow

Princess Fiona

Princie

Queenie

Robin Hood

Saint Francis

Saucer

Serf

Shrek

Spamalot

Sir Meow

Tim the Enchanter

Village Idiot

Vlad

White Knight

William the
   Conqueror

Wizard

THE MEANINGS OF THE MOST POPULAR CAT NAMES

There are still those who insist on choosing what is popular and following the trends. Cat names are constantly trending up and down, like the stock market, and often the factors involve the viral online cat business. No industry has seen larger growth, and you'll be happy to know that if you just adopted a kitten or generously provided a home for a stray, you are possibly sitting on a goldmine. To take but one example, Grumpy Cat became a superstar online and his celebrity led to endorsement deals, desk calendars, and a Lifetime Christmas movie. Grumpy actually out-earned Oprah in 2014. Understand, becoming a celebrity is one of your cat's primal instincts—like hunting for mice or birds, cats are happiest banging away at a keyboard or getting stuck in some tight-fitting tube.

And one does not get a million likes and followers overnight. It can take a whole weekend. But choosing the right name is critical and it can be one little thing that tips the scales. Changing one letter in the name, like Harry Potter to Hairy Potter, can mean the difference between feral and viral.

Should you decide to go with one of the more common names, ignoring the whole point of this book, we at least recommend choosing based on the name's origin and history:

CHAIRMAN MEOW: The go-to humorous name for cat owners who think they thought of it first, Chairman Meow is Mandarin in origin. The word *meow* was first used to represent a cat sound in 1842. The words used for cat sounds before that included *meaw*, *miaow*, and *miau* dating back to the 1630s. *Miau* means "cat" in Chinese and coincidentally, *Mao* means "cat" in Mandarin.

CHARLIE: Of English origin meaning "free man," Charlie is one of the most popular unisex names today after a 50-year plus absence. This has meant a lot; Brooklyn and Hollywood hipsters like Rebecca Romijn have named their babies Charlie. Charlie is a gateway to using hyphens. Cats need love and affection, not hyphens.

CUDDLES: This is a unisex name that means to "come together." It is in fact not British nor related to The Beatles but Irish in origin and traced back to the word *snug* (1687) or *snuggle*. It is a variant of the Irish cat name *McCuddles* and not to be confused with *McLitter*.

FELIX: The name Felix is a boy's name of Latin origin meaning "happy, fortunate," originally a Roman surname meaning blessed with luck by the gods. You know who is not that lucky? Everyone named Felix. Only Adolf has more negative connotations, thanks to Felix The Cat and finicky Felix Unger, both fictional characters that are equally annoying.

FINN: The name Finn is a good name for a white male cat because it's a boy's name of Irish origin meaning "fair or white." Finn was the name of the greatest hero of Irish mythology, Finn MacCool (aka Fionn mac Cuumhaill). MacCool has the superpowers of smarts, generosity, and the coolest name there is. Super cool couple Christy Turlington and Ed Burns named their son Finn (not MacCool). But naming your cat Finn OR MacCool is a good choice.

FLUFFY: The name Fluffy comes from the root word *fluff* and means "containing or resembling fluff." First appeared in use in 1825. There is no truth to any James Bond villains naming their cats Fluffy, although public perception would have one think otherwise. While there have been films, bands, and even footwear named Fluffy, there are absolutely no military leaders, presidents, or popes named Fluffy in history. In the arts, there are no great painters, composers, or great writers with the name either. Only after *Harry Potter* did the name become predominant, despite its being such a popular cat name for so long.

FRISKY: The word *frisky* dates back to 1500s Middle England and means lively, "gaily active." The root of Frisky is *frisk*, based on the Old French word *frisque*. Frisky often means playful when referring to animals but is sometimes used when humans are acting affectionate and animal-like. Like the security guards at airport customs who tell you they need to "frisk" you. Frisky became a popular cat name when a major cat food company started with the same name.

KITTY: The name Kitty is English for "pure" and has been used as a kitten's name since 1719. It was a common nickname in the eighteenth century for any Katherines, Kathys, or Katies.

Kitty was a character in both *Pride and Prejudice* and Dickens's *Bleak House*. There was also a Miss Kitty in *Gunsmoke*, a Kitty on *That 70's Show*, and one of the X-Men. The Wright brothers made their first historic flight at Kitty Hawk, North Carolina. It began being used as slang for a pool of money in poker in 1884.

But Kitty is the most popular car name with cat-burglars. Almost every movie scene with someone breaking into a home the line is, "Here, Kitty, Kitty . . . " Here, Kitty, Kitty is also the name of a board game.

LEO: It's a Zodiac sign, so it's always been a popular name for cats among New Agers dating back thousands and thousands of years in ancient Mayan civilizations . . . and Brooklyn. German with a Latin origin of "lion," 13 popes have had the name Leo, including St. Leo the Great. The name is enjoying a resurgence, partly to do with Leonardo "Leo" DiCaprio. As a result, Penelope Cruz and Javier Bardem named their son Leo, as did NASCAR driver Jeff Gordon. It's unclear if a lot of cats were named Leo during the time of Leonardo da Vinci, or even if any of da Vinci's buddies called him Leo.

LUCY: The name Lucy (or Luci and Lucie) is Latin for "light," from the word *lux*. Lucy is used as both a saint's name and a heroine's name in many great novels. We know the name from recent pop culture because of the *Peanuts* cartoon character Lucy, The Beatles' "Lucy in the Sky with Diamonds," the adored TV show *I Love Lucy*, and the American activist Lucy Stone.

MOLLY: The name Molly is Hebrew for "bitter." It started as a pet name for Mary in the Middle Ages. There have been many Mollys in history; the Molly Maguires, Molly Goldberg, the Revolutionary War heroine Molly Pitcher, Molly Ringwald, Molly Bloom (from James Joyce's *Ulysses*), and "Good Golly, Miss Molly" by Little Richard. It should be also noted that it is a common slang word for the drug Ecstasy, a female know-it-all, or Miss Perfect.

OSCAR: This is a boy's name of English and Irish origin, meaning "deer-lover or champion warrior." In Irish legend, Oscar was one of the greatest warriors and the grandson of Finn Mac Cumhaill. Yes, we're back to Mac-Cool again. No name has a more spectacular range of different famous representations: Oscar Wilde, *The Odd Couple's* Oscar Madison, Oscar Hammerstein, Oscar Peterson, Oscar de la Renta, and *Sesame Street's* Oscar the Grouch. But why is Hollywood's most coveted award named the Oscar? Academy employees had begun nicknaming the trophies Oscars after an executive secretary there said in 1931 that the statuette reminded her of her "Uncle Oscar." Oscar Hammerstein won an Oscar twice for Best Original Song.

SIMBA: The name Simba is a boy's name of Swahili origin meaning "lion" or "strength," made popular in the Western world because of Walt Disney's *The Lion King*. It was only after its release in 1994 that the name become so popular for both cat AND dog owners. Simba was inspired by Disney's 1942 *Bambi* combined with Moses and the Bible and even Hamlet. I suppose one could duplicate the iconic character in *Lion King* by holding your new kitten over your head out over your kitchen patio or front porch. A petition was made for the Duchess of Cambridge, Kate Middleton, and Prince William to hold their newborn this way at Buckingham Palace in July 2013. Perhaps it was too soon after Michael Jackson dangled a baby off a Berlin balcony in 2002.

SOCKS: The word *sock* is from early fourteenth-century England, meaning "light shoe or slipper." The Latin word *soccus* means "low-heeled shoe." Experts believe that it derives from the Greek *sykchos* but may be of Phrygian origin. Immensely more interesting, in the 1950s began the slang sock hop for dances where attendees take off their shoes.

The connection between socks and cats' fascination with balls of yarn is that socks are knitted. Cats don't actually love balls of yarn as much as they are trying to defeat them. Zoologists claim that a cat's primal hunting instincts attract it to anything that dangles and moves around in a manner vaguely resembling that of a mouse or bird. They think unwinding yarn is a snake. Yarn's light weight and inability to strike back make it a cat's perfect prey and easy for them to bat around with their paws. I try to warn cat-owners and knitters, there are centuries of lion DNA in every cat waiting for you to turn your back. Their lack of logic and overpowering natural instincts prevent cats from getting it into their tiny brains that the ball of yarn is not threatening them, no matter how many times they return to it.

What can you do? Well, for starters, when you move yourself, don't "untangle" or mimic snake-like motions. Don't roll across the room. If you don't believe me, try it.

Secondly, do not allow cats to play with balls of yarn. It can present serious health problems for cats, and it's important to discuss the risks. Cats can choke on yarn. I'm not referring to a small noose, although tiny tails or legs can get twisted in the yarn resulting in hanging from an unfinished sweater or winter cap. But cats can choke if they try eating the yarn. Swallowing yarn can be even more dangerous, obstructing their delicate digestive tracts. Signs can include cats vomiting yarn or seeing disgusting yarn in the litter box.

So replace balls of yarn with professionally engineered cat toys and safe ball-of-yarn substitutes. There are actually companies, like I Can't Believe It's Not Wool and Feline Friendly, Inc., that make fake balls of yarn for cats. Use a yarn bowl to protect your yarn and cat and, when possible, do not knit in front of cats. Yarn bowls are found on sites like Etsy and at your finer craft fairs.

STELLA: The name Stella is a girl's name of Latin origin meaning "star." It was the name of the character in Sir Philip Sidney's 1590 poem, "Astrophel and Stella." Stella made pop culture fame when, in *A Streetcar Named Desire,* Marlon Brando screamed the name from the street, although he was not calling for a cat. This was followed up by Sir Paul McCartney's daughter, Stella, becoming a world-famous fashion designer.

TABBY: The word *tabby* is French, from *tabis*, or "a rich, watered silk," an adjective from the 1630s originating in Baghdad and later used for cats with striped coats. Tabbies are known as domestic cats with an M marking on their foreheads. Both cartoons Heathcliff and Garfield are tabbies. Tabbies are notorious for being intelligent and affectionate if not often moody. And no *type* of cat (not using the word *breed* as tabbies are not a breed) is better at resolving a mouse problem.

The most fascinating thing cats do is bring their catch, dead or alive, back to you as a gift. Some cats gather toys and objects in the middle of the night so that they are waiting for you. They are instinctively pack animals, so they want to share with their "family" what they caught or found. So foremost, it's a compliment; they consider you family. Like at the Olive Garden. Measures to take to prevent having live and dead birds and chipmunks brought to your bedside include playing with your cat and getting some of that desire out of their system. Adding bells to their collars to warn wildlife of oncoming shenanigans can help, too. Lasers and stuffed toy animals satisfy many of their hunter tendencies, as well.

TIGER: Tiger Woods' real first name is Eldrick (I've never heard of a cat named Eldrick), ushering in a period of time when animal names like Fox, Wolf, or Ferret have become stylish names for both baby boys and pets. Tiger has become so synonymous with the golfer that it has become overexposed, like the names Bob or Joe or Billy Joel. We would discourage the use of the name Tiger (or Eldrick) unless your cat has a history of driving mishaps in SUVs.

WHISKERS: A whisker was a word first used to describe animal lip hair in the 1670s. 1839 is the date of the first specific reference to cat whiskers.

Cat whiskers serve many important functions. These natural antennae provide additional sensory data regarding movement and objects, allowing cats to navigate their environment. Cats use their whiskers to determine space and can decide on whether they can squeeze into narrow spaces, like between furniture or holes in a fence. Whiskers can also detect air and objects, helping them locate toys and food bowls in the dark. Proprioceptors at the ends of the whiskers improve balance and control the position of their legs and body, which is why cats always land on their feet.

For all these reasons I have let my own whiskers grow. Ear and nose hair, while disgusting, has helped me find my own toys and improved my balance. I get my car keys and wallet faster and not so much walk but sashay now. I have found I get stuck less frequently as well. Take a break from personal grooming and see if you don't notice a difference.

The Next Huge TikTok Star

bob

CATS NAMED AFTER FAMOUS PEOPLE IN HISTORY

Sometimes you just know when a cat is destined for greatness. And on rare occasions this cat reminds you of someone famous. By naming your cat after someone famous, you are convincing others, subconsciously, that your cat possesses some of that person's attributes. Other cats will treat your cat better, too.

Aaron Purr

Alexander the Great

Annie Oakley

Caesar

Catherine the Great

Cat

Charlie Brown

Columbus

Copernicus

Darwin

Edith Piaf

Eric the Red

Fluffy Madison

Fuzz Aldrin

Galilei

Gandhi

George Pawshington

Henry Hissinger

Jackie O

Kennedy

Lady Di

Lucky Lindberg

Lucky Lindy

Malcolm

Marco Polo

Margaret Scratcher

Maximilian

Notorious R.B.G.

Pocahontas

Princess Di

Roosevelt

Tabby Roosevelt

Truman

Wright Brothers

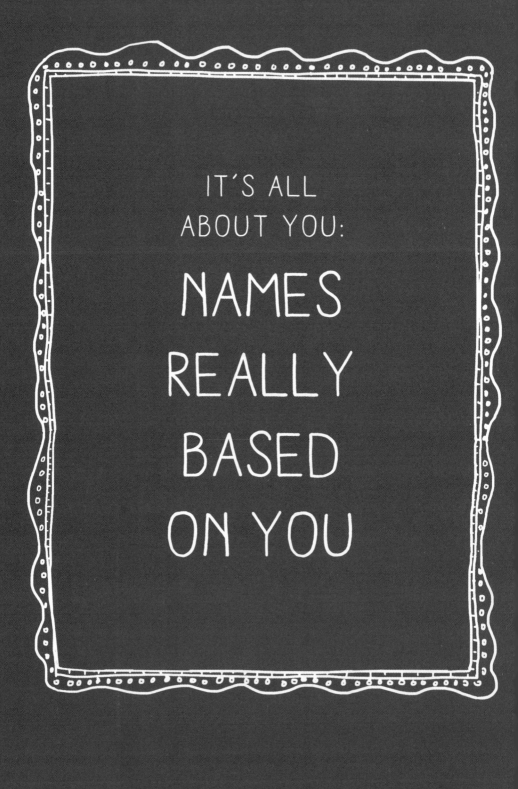

IT'S ALL
ABOUT YOU:

NAMES

REALLY

BASED

ON YOU

LET'S ASSUME FOR A MOMENT THAT CATS

could care less what you named them. Maybe the cat simply doesn't care what we name it. It's possible. But not all bets are off. You still have to name it something, if for no other reason than to clarify that you are talking to the cat if there is someone else in the room. You are going to trick your cat into caring by making its name all about you, thus making your pet sit up and care because now he or she finds itself saddled with a name that comes out of left field.

Perhaps this book was putting too much pressure on you to choose the perfect name. Let's ratchet it back a bit. Having realistic low expectations could probably save you a lot of aggravation and help you cope with your inevitable disappointment with your pet's total apathy. The hell with the cat. This chapter is about you. You deserve a little attention. So far, it's been all cats, cats, cats. You're the one who's great. You got a cat. And you have been stuck with all the heavy lifting.

NAMES FOR KITTENS YOU PLAN TO USE TO ATTRACT A PARTNER

There is nothing wrong with using your pet to attract a person of your dreams, given that your pet IS a part of you. You are being given permission, here and now, our blessing, to increase your chances of finding your mate, even if that means pushing a shopping cart of kittens in the middle of the Great Lawn at Central Park—the oldest trick in the book. Not this book, per se, but "the" book.

Angel	Magic	Tax Shelter
Blue Eyes	Mr. Right	Tiger
Downtown	Slowhand	Wild Cat
Lucky	Soapy	Woody

CAT NAMES FOR ART LOVERS

Art lovers and cat lovers are people of great taste and sophistication. You must let other people know how smart and stylish you are by giving your cat a name displaying just that: great taste and sophistication. Felix the Cat is not going to cut it.

Andy Hairball	Frida	Salvador Deli
Banksy	Jackson Haddoc	Toulouse-Pawtec
Bobcat Ross	Leonardo da Whiskers	Whiskers Mother
Doodle	Mona Lisa	
Figaro	Pablo Peecasso	

NAMES IF YOU ARE ALLERGIC TO YOUR CAT

Allergy	Flakes	Sneezes
Dandelion	Hives	Sudafed
Dander	Itchy	Patches
Dandruff	Mr. Runny Eyes	Spots
EpiPen	Rash	Wheezer

CAT OWNERS WHO ARE DOCTORS

Is there anything cuter than a cat with a doctor's name? Hearing over the intercom in a waiting room, "Dr. Pudding? Dr. Pudding?" and then seeing a fluffy cat strut by is funny. Laughter is indeed the best medicine, not counting support cats. If you are a physician; chiropractor; ears, nose, and throat specialist; neurologist; psychiatrist; or any kind of medical professor, you'll want to seriously give the following list a check-up.

"And how does that make you feel?"

Catheter
Cat Scan
Cuddles, M.D.
Dr. Bigglesworth
Dr. Bob Hartley
Dr. Caligari
Dr. Doolittle
Dr. Doug Ross
Dr. Emmett Brown
Dr. Fauci
Dr. Feelgood
Dr. Frankenstein
Dr. Fu Manchu
Dr. Giggles
Dr. Goldfoot

Dr. Jekyll
Dr. Katz
Dr. Kildare
Dr. Leonard McCoy
Dr. Love
Dr. Moreau
Dr. Oz
Dr. Pepper
Dr. Pudding
Dr. Quinn
Dr. Tinkle
Dr. Vinnie Boombotz
Dr. Who
Dr. Yuri Zhivago
Dr. Zachary Smith

Doozie
Frasier
Hawkeye
Hot Lips
Lab Rat
Marcus Welby
Measles
Nurse Jackie
PMS
Quincy
Rabies
Salk
Trapper
Vasectomy

NAMES FOR CAT OWNERS WHO ARE LAWYERS

All I want to say is Paw & Disorder. Let's get straight to it and suggest names for pets that are legalistic.

Alley Cat Beal
Bailiff
Catlock
Docket
Erin Scratchovich
Jacoby & Meyers

Habeas Corpus
Hostile Witness
Judge Kibble
Judge Whiskers
Libel
Mr. Rebuttal

My Cousin Furry
 (court mobster)
Purry Mason
Ruth Bader Catsberg

"Judge, may the records show how cute this kitty is."

CATS NAMED ONLY FOR NO OTHER REASON THAN BECAUSE NOW YOU'RE ON LEGALIZED MARIJUANA

For the record, I don't condone drug use unless it is recommended by your vet. I also find drug humor beneath me, but this list just kept getting funnier and funnier, so I had no choice.

Alice B. Toke-las	Doobie	Rose Marie
Baked	Greta	Scoobie
Blunt	Hashie	Sinister Minister
Bobo Bush	Hooch	Snoop Dog
Burnie	Mr. Green	Stash
Catnip	Mary Jane	Stogie
Cheeba	Poppy	Stoner
Cheech	Pretendo	Whacky Tabacky
Clam Bake	Reefer	Zoo Wee Mama
Dinking Dow	Reverend Green	

NAMES FOR EMOTIONAL SUPPORT CATS

Angel

Clara Burton

Dr. Katz

Dr. Phil

Dependent

Doc

Florence
  Nightingale

Frasier

Mood Swing

Moody

My Cry Pillow

MyPlusOne

Nurse Jackie

Nursie

Pity Kitty

Shrink

Sigmund Furry

Support Cat

"Worst. Emotional. Support. Cat. Ever."

NAMES FOR PATRIOTIC OWNERS

God bless America. God bless your cat. If you are someone who has dressed your cat up at some time as Uncle Sam or the Statue of Liberty and posted it on the internet, and you know who you are, then this list is for you.

Abe

Admiral

Allegiance

Apple Pie

Betty

Blue

Comeback Kid	Honest Abe	Paw Revere
Coolidge	Liberty	Philadelphia
D.C.	Lincoln	Pioneer
Democracy	Mayflower	Plymouth
Dreamer	Monticello	President Furrball
Eisenhower	JFK	Quincy
FDR	Jackie	Roosevelt
Freedom	John F. Kitty	Scranton
Gettysburg	Katala Harris	Smithsonian
Glory	Kennedy	Truman
Hairy Truman	Kit Carson	Uncle Sam
Hero	Kitty Van Buren	Victory

CAT NAMES BASED ON YOUR FAVORITE MOVIE

Apocalypse Meow	Fur Ball Express	Pink Panther
Catablanca	Goodfella	Purrple Rain
Catman	The Graduate	Scarface
Coconuts	Hairy Potter	Single White Feline
Dirty Hairy	Indy Jones	Tabby McGuire
Eraserhead	Jaws	Tarzan

CAT NAMES FOR FOODIES

Are you a foodie? Then this is an excellent list for you to peruse. If you are not sure you are a foodie, ask a friend. They will be able to tell you. Suppose you enjoy cooking classes, you have a scrapbook of your meals, your refrigerator has its own Instagram account, and you are a nightmare to make dinner plans with. Sound right? Then read on, because you will also be very particular about your cat's name.

Chef	Tony the Tiger
Foodie	Tubby
Spoons	Wolfgang

Although these are some delicious suggestions, this is really an area where you should come up with the name on your own. There are end-less subCATegories under the umbrella of food names that can send you down a rabbit hole (that's hasenpfeffer for foodies). You can name your cat after any favorite restaurant or dish, but to help inspire you, here are some suggestions divided into main areas on the food pyramid to get you started.

MEATS

Chorizo	Kabob	_____
Felino	Pepperino	_____
Genoa	Pork Chop	_____

CARBS

Biscuit	Crumpets	Donut
Butter	Cupcake	Dumplings

Mochi	Spaghetti	_____
Muffins	Teddy Spaghetti	_____
Shortcake	Waffles	_____

SNACKS

Cheeto	Kit Kat	Pop-Tart
Chocolate	Lollipop	Pudding
Cinnamon	Mr. Snacks	_____
Cocoa	Macaron	_____
Cookie	Marshmallow	_____
Fudge	S'more	_____
Jellybean	Pop'n Fresh	_____

FRUITS & VEGETABLES

Beans	Pepper	Turnip
Capers	Pickles	Yammie (orange tabby)
Coconuts	Pumpkin	_____
Lemon	Squash	_____
Mango	Sweet Pea	_____
Olive	Tater	_____
Peanut Butter	Truffles	_____

DAIRY

Brie	Feta	Stilton
Caerphilly	Gouda	Velveeta
Camembert	Halloumi	_____
Cheshire	Manchego	_____
Edam	Mascarpone	_____
Emmental	Roquefort	_____
Epoisses	Romano	_____

LOOKS
AND
MANNERS

SERIOUSLY, WHEN DID NAMING A CAT BECOME

so hard? I think maybe we are overthinking this a bit. Let's return to basics. Look at your new kitten and say out loud what you see. No, go on, put down this book and stare into those eyes.

Hopefully you came back to find out what to do next. Okay, what did you see? Look for the list below that matches your cat.

NAMES FOR CUTE KITTENS SO CUTE YOU'RE ABOUT TO BURST

Sometimes a cat is so precious it needs its own special list of names. But no list in this book requires more thought or has such huge consequences. You need to remember that you will have to use this name constantly, every day, and often in public. Some of these names are nauseating. To ensure you pick a name you can live with for many happy years to come, we strongly suggest you proceed with caution and not make a final decision without testing the selection first: If you can't repeat the name out loud ten times in a row without bursting into laughter or cringing, move on to something else.

Baby Bumble

Beep Boop

Bimbles

Bimbly

Blinky

Blossom

Boo Boo

Boobyhead

Boopsie

Bootsy

Bubbles

Bumbilicious

Bumble Baby

Bumble Bear

Bumble Boy

Bumble O Bumbles

Bumbles

Bumbles, Senior

Bumbly

Bumplings

Bundles

Butterball

Crumbles

Crumbly

Cuddlebug

Cuddles

Cupcake

Dumbly

Dumplings

Fluffy

Frosting

Fruit Loops

Goggles

Goosebump

Gumdrop

Hiccup

Honey Boo Boo

Humbles

Jiggles

Juggles

Jumbles

Main Muffin

Marbles

McBumbles

Mittens

Miss Bumbles

Potsy

Rumbles

Schlumbles

Sir Bumbles

Snookums

Sprinkles	Tumbles	Wimpies
Stumbles	Waffles	Zsa Zsa
Teacup	Wiggles	

NAMES FOR BLACK CATS

There are over twenty-two different breeds of black cats and all of them are bad luck. Or so some people may believe. Black cats have always been associated with superstitions, but many of those are good. In Scotland a strange black cat's arrival at the home means prosperity. In Japan, a lady who owns a black cat will have many suitors. In Germany, some believe that a black cat crossing a person's path from left to right means favorable times. At sea, sailors have always considered black cats lucky.

Black Cat Appreciation Day is August 17 in the United States, and it's Black Cat Day on October 27 in the UK. This information is meant to encourage people from adopting black cats, who can be difficult to find a home for.

Ashes	Eight Ball	Michael Ian Black
Black Panther	Espresso	Shadow
Charcoal	Flint	Smokey
Darth Vader	Fudge	Smudge
Earl Grey	Lewis Black	

NAMES FOR WHITE CATS

Don't make the same mistake so many people have made, calling their white cat an obvious cliché name, only to regret it the rest of that pet's life. Give your cat some pizzazz, some originality, with one of these unanticipated names you will regret for the rest of that pet's life.

Anderson Pooper

Angel

Aspirin

Avalanche

Casper

Chalk

Cotton Ball

Marshmallow

Mayonnaise

Puss

Sir Coconut

Snowball

Snowy

NAMES FOR DIFFICULT CATS

Let's face it, most cats are difficult. They deserve a name that fits how much they make you endure. It's actually part of the healing process and a form of stress relief if you're able to scream, "Hey, Grumpy Cat" a few times a day instead of, let's say, "Hey, Mr. Easy-Going."

Abominable

Attila the Fun

Bad Cat-titude

Bad Kitty

Bam Bam

The Beast from the
 East

Bruiser

Catzilla

Chairman of the
 Bored

Crooked Nose Jack

Dr. Fart

Destroyer

Doomsday

Fat Tony

Gangrene

Genghis Khan

Gravedigger

Heart Break Kitten

The Impaler

Ivan The Terrible

Jaws

Kerfuffle

Killer

Killer Kowalski

Kitty of Darkness

"You still just play with yarn?"

Krazy Kat

Little Rocket Man

Love Bites

Mr. Boss

Mr. Stoic

Mr. Warmth

Mad Max

Madcap

Menace

Miss Aloof

Miss Kapooffnik

Mischief Maker

Napoleon

Nasty

Nicotine Patches

Pretty Boy Floyd

Prince of Darkness

Reboots

Ruffian

Scoundrel

Scratches

Scuffs

Snow Kitty

Sofa Killer

Stalin

Stonewall

Stormy

Sylvester

Thor

Toxic

Un FURtunate

Wild Thing

MUSICAL CATS

Have you noticed your cat displaying a special aptitude for rhythm? Or have you caught him or her lip-syncing to the radio? These are the foundations of the meme industry.

Hit songs about cats include *The Year of the Cat*, *The Lion Sleeps Tonight*, *Cat On a Hot Tin Roof*, Tom Jones' *What's New Pussycat?*, Squeeze's *Cool For Cats*, The Cure's *Lovecats*, The Stray Cats' *Stray Cat Strut*, Harry Chapin's *Cat In The Cradle*, Ted Nugent's *Cat Scratch Fever* . . . and yet not one hit song about cats from musician Cat Stevens. Ummm.

Here are some names if you and/or your cat is musical.

Adele	Bojangles	D.J.
Beverly Window Sills	Bono	Eminem
The Big Bopper	Bruce	Fifth Beatle
Bing Clawsby	Cat Benatar	Hairy Connick Jr.
Black-Eyed Pea	Cats Domino	Honky Tonk Cat
The Boss	Catsy Cline	Kitty Perry

Lady Gaga

Liberace

Lorde

Madonna

Marley

Mick Jaguar

Mr. Blue Skies

Notorious C.A.T.

Ol' Blue Eyes

Otis

P. Diddy

Paw McCartney

Phenomenal Cat

Pink

Prince

Prince of Darkness

Rihanna

RuPaw

Sade

Seger

Sid Vicious

Smokey

Snoop Kitty Cat

SteppenWolf

Sting

Supertramp

The Weeknd

Wolfgang

Woodstock

Ziggy Stardust

(3 CATS):

Crosby, Stills, and
   Nash

Peter, Paul, and
   Mary

NAMES FOR SPORTY CATS

Not every cat is a lazy layabout, and sporty cats deserve a sporty name. Or maybe it would be funny and ironic to name your slothful cat something inspirational and sporty instead of going with "Comatose" or "Snail."

Any other use of these names, descriptions, or accounts of your cat without the NFL's express written consent is permissible and silly.

Air Jordan

Ali

Andre the Giant

Babe

Babolat

Bambino

Bo

Boomer

Blitz

Buckeye

Butterball Bundy

Catfish Hunter

Cecil Breeder

Champ

Cobb

Comiskey

Crazy Legs

Dr. J

DiMaggio

Eli

Feline Jones

Fenway

Flo-Jo

Fluffy Griffith Joyner

Fluffy Jean King

Gil

Gorgeous George

Indy

Joltin' Joe

Killer Kowalski

Kobe

Mr. Met

Mr. October

Magic

Marvelous Marv

Mascot

Megan Napinoe

Mickey

Nature Boy

Pee Wee

Pele

Pistol Pete

Prime Time

Prince Lombardi

Puss N Glutes

Rafa

Rocky

Satchmo

Say Hey Kid

Serena

Shoeless Joe

South Paw

Stan the Man

Swiss Miss

Tiger

Willie

Willie Mouseconi

World B. Free

Yaz

Yogi

MIDDLE NAMES FOR CATS

Boo	Kay	Meg
Kat	Kit	Rina
Kate	Kittie	Tess

GAMES TO PLAY TO COME UP WITH YOUR CAT'S NAME

Many of you out there are also game people. So why not either name your cat after your favorite game or make finding a name even more complicated than I have for you already by having to do a puzzle to find it.

Here are some game names for your cat: Scrabble, Yahtzee, Uno, Taboo, Pictionary, Boggle, Mouse Trap, Bonkers, Kerplunk, Risk, Sorry, Trouble . . . you see? These make for quite good cat names.

NAME SEARCH

E	S	O	P	H	I	E	O	G
C	H	L	O	E	O	H	R	I
M	A	X	A	Z	P	A	E	N
O	D	L	E	O	C	P	O	G
L	O	Y	L	I	L	U	E	E
L	W	B	E	I	H	M	A	R
Y	B	O	T	C	E	P	O	O
C	M	M	R	O	C	K	Y	S
A	I	L	U	C	Y	I	O	I
R	A	C	S	O	N	N	Y	E

CLUES: Moby, Racy, Lucy, Leo, Max, Sonny, Yoyo, Lily, Chloe, Shadow, Oreo, Molly, Sophie, Oscar, Mia, Gracie, Lola, Pepper, Toby, Coco, Pumpkin, Ginger, Rosie, Callie, Zoe, Rocky. *For answers, see page 100.*

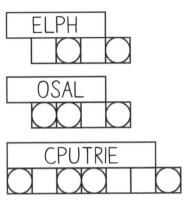

ELPH
◯◯ ◯

OSAL
◯◯◯ ◯

CPUTRIE
◯◯◯◯ ◯◯

So, are you folks...?

" ◯◯◯ ◯◯◯◯◯ "

bob

"Are you allergic to cats?"

ANSWERS: HELP, ALSO, PICTURE, "CAT PEOPLE"

NAMES
YOUR CAT
ACTUALLY
MAY ANSWER
TO

NOBODY LIKES TO BE MADE FUN OF. WITH that in mind, we are going to put aside the silliness and take the task at hand more seriously. Here in this chapter are suggestions that would make any cat as proud as a lion.

"How you got this far I'll never understand."

NAMES WITH GREAT EXPECTATIONS

Abel	God	Miss Havisham
Bentley	Kismet	Pip
Biddy	Mr. Jaggers	Princess
Duchess	Mr. Pumblechook	

NAMES THAT COMMAND RESPECT

Maybe you feel your cat not only needs a name but a promotion. Now's the time. When giving your pet a new name, make it one that commands respect, one that makes it clear to everyone in the family that your cat has the corner office and the buck stops there.

Ali

Big Cat

Duchess

Fat Tony

Her Royal Heinie

Lion

Max

MeeToo

Nostradamus

Pearl

Princess Kate

    Piddleton, aka Piddles

Ravishing

Sir Meow

Winnie

*"One day, son, this windowsill
will all be yours."*

*"Your motivation is food. You're
waiting to be fed."*

"Tonight we have on a box of kittens."

HOLLYWOOD CATS

All cats are stars (especially on the Internet), and the right name is everything. Change your Smelly Cat to a name that demands admiration and has a sense of glamour.

Anthony Purrkins
Black Panther
Bobcat Goldthwait
Boots
Botox
Cat-Nipsy Russell
Chairman of the
  Bored
Cheetah Rivera
Citizen Kat
David Litterbox
David Litterman &
  Paw Shaffer (for
  twins)
Divine Miss M
The Duke
Elwood & Jake
Engelbert
  Humperdinck
The Face
Fleas Witherspoon
The Fresh Prince
GalactiCat

Garland
Hissy Spacek
Hollywood
Howl Halbrook
Hulu
Indy Jones
It Girl
James Spayed
Jean Clawed Van
  Damm
Jimmy Kibble
Joe Bodega Cat
Kat Williams
Kat Winslet
The King of Late-
  Night
Kristie Alley Cat
Kitten Kardashian
Laurence Fishbone
Leonardo de
  CatNapio
The Little Tramp
Lucille Furball

Lucy
Meow Farrow
Michael Dogless
Minnie
Mr. Warmth
Miss Piggy
Nicole Kitman
Patrick Fluffy
Purrscilla Presley
Radar
Shatner
Shrek
Smurf
Spike Flea
Spock
Sundance Kid
Sylvester
Tabby McGuire
Tarzan
Tinkerbelle
Tony
Will Feral

IF YOU
SUSPECT
YOUR CAT
CAN READ

IT DOES SEEM LIKE CATS ARE ALWAYS

hanging around near books. Of course, this is just a coincidence but it does remind one again of that age-old question: who's smarter, cats or dogs? (Everyone thinks cats, so it's actually not much of a thought-provoking query. This is mostly the fault of a few dumb dogs online giving them a bad name.)

It *would* be great if cats could read, I suppose. Alas, I can only dream of getting blurbs and reviews for this book from actual cats. But I say *suppose* because I'm assuming the reviews would be good. So, the lesson there is that you have to watch what you wish for. But it would be fun to speculate what books would be a cat's favorite books to read. Probably cookbooks. And maybe knitting books and murder mysteries.

bob

WRITER'S BLOCK

LIBRARY CATS

Alicia Hull

Barbara Gordon

Bookmark

Buffy

Bunny Watson

Dewey

Late Fee

Librarian

Lion

Marian Paroo

Stack

Bestsellers

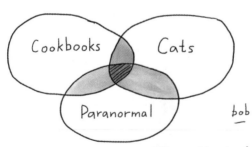

bob

▨ Cookbooks for cats with nine lives

NAMES FOR *VERY* SMART CATS

Cat owners are quick to say that cats are more intelligent than dogs. There is no scientific basis for this claim besides hundreds of viral videos making a case against both sides. However, there are some cat owners who will swear their kitten is *gifted*. For those special cats we have a special list of names for *very* smart cats.

Big Nap Theory

Desiderius Erasmouse

E = MC Clawed

EinStain

Egghead

Elon Musk

Gigabyte

Guru

Lego

Leonardo da Whiskers

Madame Purrie

Poindexter

Princeton

RBG

Stephen Pawkins

Toonces, the Driving Cat

Witty Kitty

Wiz Kid

Wonder Woman

bob

BOOKSTORE CATS

Ahh, the bookstore cat. There is nothing like the elegant and mysterious bookstore cat who lurks between the aisles to remind you, "This is not a library . . . oh, and please feed me . . ." A cat of this upper-crust standing in the feline world deserves an equally distinguished name.

Abel Shufflebottom

Atticus Finch

Bard of Avon

Bentley

Biddy

Champ

Charles Lickings

Charlotte Bronte

Dickens

Downton Tabby

e. e. cummings

Edgar Allen Paw

Emily Whiskerson

Eustace Tilley

François Féline

The Great Catsby

Heathcliff

Herodotus

Holmes

Homer

Jane Austen

Leo Chew-Toy

Mr. Jaggers

Mr. Pumblechook

Mark Twine

Minimus

Miss Havisham

Norman Meower

Oscar Wildcat

Papa Hemingway

Pip

The Prince

Purradise Lost

Shakespaw

T.S. Belliot

"Why do you suppose so many bestsellers are cat books?"

BOOKSTORE CATS PART II

Let's admit it. If you are a cat lover, you're picky. And our cats are even pickier than us, so we are going to break down the bookstore cats by where you would likely found them perusing their book genre of choice. (See above for the classics.)

NONFICTION

David Foster Whiskers   Meow Angelou   Walden

Frank McCat   Play-toy   Yeats

Jonathan Swift   Truman Catpote

CHILDREN'S AND YA

Adrian Mole   Hairy Potter   Peter Rabbit

Cheshire Cat   J.K. Meowling   Tootle

Dr. Seuss   Katniss   Very Hungry Cat

FanCat   The Outsider

SCIENCE FICTION

451

Cat Sagan

Cat's Cradle

George Hairball

H. P. Wells

Handmaid

The Thing

"Take us to your litter box."

ROMANCE

Danielle Still	Midnight	Sparks
E.L. Cat	Prince Charming	White Knight

SELF-HELP

Badass	Deepak Cat	Suze Orman
Chicken Soup	The Secret	

MYSTERY

Cat on the Train	Da Vinci Cat	Miss Marple
Cat with a Dragon Tattoo	Dupin	Sir Arthur Conan Doyle
	Gone Kitty	

NAMES THAT ARE HARD TO REMEMBER

You walk into a new friend's home, and they start introducing their cats: Ruby, Maddy Mister Sophie II, Nimbus, Teddy Spaghetti, Imperator Publius Aelius Hadrianus, Affectionate Mew . . . whoo, whoo, whoo. Hold it right there, I need a pen and paper. Remembering a cat's name shouldn't be homework. You know the type: this is the friend who must do everything the different and difficult way. Deciding where to eat with a group requires a Senate hearing; they insist cauliflower pizza tastes like other pizza; in your book club, they pick a book not available anywhere, only to learn it hasn't been written yet; their Halloween costume requires a 30-minute explanation. For them, nothing less than an off-the-wall name for your cat will do.

Thanks to hiss-terical stand-up comedian Eddie Izzard, here are fourteen names sure to trip up anyone plus get your cat's attention. The British comedian once said, "Cats have a scam going—you buy the food, they eat the food, they go away; that's the deal."

Wingelbert	Zengelbert	Dindlebert Zindledack
Humptyback	Bingledack	Engelbert
Soup Bunwalla	Zingelbert	Humptyback
Kringelbert	Bembledack	Engelbert
Fishtybuns	Yingybert	Humperdinck
Steviebuns	Dambleban	Vingelbert
Bottrittrundle	Zangelbert	Wingledanck
Tringelbert	Bingledack	Engelbert Slaptyback
Wangledack	Klingybun Fistelvase	

NAMES YOU WOULD THINK YOUR CAT CAN PRONOUNCE

All cat owners wish their cat could talk. And say their own name. Maybe meeting them halfway with names they can almost pronounce now is the closest you will come to that dream.

Mao	Ech	Noel
Maya	Hissy	Oeew
Merle	Lester Sneeze	Raul
Mia	Nala	Squeaks

GRATUITOUS STRAYS & RESCUES

THERE WAS ONCE A TIME WHEN KITTENS

arrived at one's doorstep in a woven basket with warm muffins. Not the case anymore. Kittens are often thrust on you without warning, like your family springing on you for your hoarding problem, even after you already said you kicked your eBay habit years ago. Slithering kittens approach you in big city alleyways or pastoral farms, with adorable meows that are irresistible, making it impossible for you to say no. You're made of flesh and blood, after all.

Of course, there are also animal shelters and neighborhood grandmas trying to find a loving home for kittens that are going to think you are the cat's pajamas. For all these strays and rescues, let's give these cats a name that reflects their roots and hometown.

NEW YORK CITY CATS

There are over 3 trillion cats in New York City alone.* But there's no question that New York City cats have their own attitude and swagger. Whether you live in New York City or just love New York City, the proper name can give your cat a New York State of mind.

Apollo	Chelsea	Guggenheim
Astor	Cloudy	Harlem
Avenue	Columbus	Heckler
Backfire	Courtney	Herald
Bagel	Darby	Highline
Bakery	Deli	Highrise
Bergdorf	Downtown	Hipster
Beverly	Dude	Hudson
Birdie	Duke	Intrepid
Bodega	Duplex	JFK
Borough	Earl	Jewels
Boyfriend	Eden	Lanie
Boystown	Espresso	Lexy
Brooklyn	Everything	Mr. Big
Bronx Bomber	Fordham	Macy
Bryant	Freeway	Madeline
Cabby	Frick	Madison
Carrie	Gabby	Magnolia
Chandler	Geneva	Metropolitan
Charlotte	Gridlock	Myrtle

---

* Just a wild guesstimate based on my building.

Nordstrom

Nutcracker

Odessa

Open Mic

Piano Man

Rockaway

Rockefeller

Rockette

Rush Hour

Schlep

Schmear

Shortie

Sidewalk

Skyline

Subway

Taxi

Times Square

Tourist

Traffic

Tramp

bob

Transplant

Tribune

Tunnel

Whitney

Williams Burg

York

Click Bait For Cats

**Top Ten Places
To Do Nothing**

**Scientists Discover
World's Largest
Fur Ball**

**How To Drive
a Couple
Crazy in Bed**

bob

LOS ANGELES CATS

A cat's name has to reflect their personality, and there is no bigger contrast between personalities than between East Coast and West Coast cats. If you thought cats were laid back, hang out one weekend with an LA cat. It's 24-7 partying . . . and napping. Here are some great monikers for West Coast cats.

Agent	Kale	Pilot
Beverly	Kaley	Santa Monica
Botox	La Brea	Selfie
Dodger	Lax	Smoothie
Freeway	Malibu	Spin-off
Grammy	Pacific	Surfer
Heatwave	Pedro	Traffic
Hermosa	Peloton	
Jim Morrison	Pilates	

CHICAGO CATS

Somehow cat owners in the Midway caught wind that LA and NYC cats were getting love in this book and not them. Well, not so. Here are some Windy City–centric names.

Al Catpone	Dillinger	Second Kitty
Butkus	Ernie Banks	Vienna Red
Cub	Frank Lloyd Cat	White Sox
Da Bear	Gold Coast	Windy
Deep Dish	Leo Durocher	Wrigley
Dempster	Loopy	

LAS VEGAS CATS

Nobody comes home from Las Vegas with a new cat. I haven't heard of one incident. But we did do cat names for New York, LA, and Chicago. And fair is fair. Vegas IS our country's most popular tourist destination. And gambling terminology lends itself, actually, to some really cool cat names. So for the gamblers out there, maybe what you find in Vegas DOESN'T need to stay in Vegas.

21	Casino	Fremont
Ante	Chips	The Gambler
Bellagio	Comps	High Roller
Bixby	The Cooler	Mirage
Blackjack	Craps	Neon
Buffet	Double D	Roulette
Caribbean Stud	Double Down	Snake Eyes

NAMES FOR BAR CATS

One of the great ways to name a cat is naming it after where it came from. While animal shelters are still the most common places one adopts a kitten, if you are driving in the country, there is a good chance you will pass a farm with the sign, "Free Kittens." Barn cats are quite valuable to farmers and they treat cats like casual workers who need to earn their keep by killing rodents. As mentioned earlier, this has been going on for thousands of years. The best mousers are female cats who are nursing a litter (neutered cats are next to useless for mousing). Cats hunt sometimes for food and sometimes for sport; if you feed them, they will kill more mice because they have more energy for this sport. But again, in the name business, one letter makes a world of difference and let's say, for argument's sake, you never go to *barns* but frequent *bars*. Here are some great names to use if you picked up your kitten in a bar instead.

Alley Cat	Mary Pickford	Saucey
Blotto	Moonshine	Speakeasy
Bubbles	Night Owl	Tipsy
Drunk Cat	Norm	Tomcat
Hair of the Cat	Party Animal	W.C.
Hangover	Pub Cat	White Lady
The Happy Hooker	Pukesy	
Last Call	Punchline	

NAMING YOUR CAT AFTER YOUR USUAL

Baby Guinness

Bahama Mama

Bailey's

Black Velvet

Bobby Burns

Boilermaker

Bourbon Lancer

Brady

Budweiser

Cat-tail

Churchill

Daiquiri

Duck Fart

Flaming Doctor
 Pepper

Fluffy Critter

Fluffy Duck

Foster

Furnell

Fuzzy Navel

Ginny

Grasshopper

Grog

Hanky Panky

Hugo

Jack & Coke (for
 pairs)

Juan Collins

Lime Rickey

Mai Tail

Manhattan

Martini

Mint Julep

Monitor

My Fair Lady

Nutcracker

Pina Colada

Prince of Wales

Redheaded Slut

Rob Roy

Ruby Dutchess

Rummy

Scotch & Soda (for
 pairs)

Snakebite

Snowball

Spritzer

Tequila

Tipsy

Toddy

Tom Collins

Tuxedo

Vermouth

Whisker Mac

Zombie

"What part of neutered don't you understand?"

THE SUB GROUP OF VODKA

As you can see, we had to stop coming up with names for cats based on alcoholic drinks, as we would have wound up with 200 pages of just cocktails, turning this into a drink book instead of a cat book. We decided to just pick one specific type of drink and end it there. So here are some names inspired by the potable potion, vodka.

Black Russian	Kamikaze	Salty Cat
Bloody Mary	Kremlin Colonel	Screwdriver
Brass Monkey	Lemon Drop	Vesper
Caesar	Moscow Mule	Whisker
Chi-Chi	Orange Tundra	White Russian
Dirty Shirley	Paralyzer	Woo Woo
Flirtini	Platinum Blonde	
Harvey Wallbanger	Red Russian	

RELATIONSHIP QUIZ ♥ 🐾

Sounds like you are spending a lot of time in bars, single and with a cat with no name. Maybe it's time for an introspective test that begs this question: who stays, your cat or your other significant other? Choosing one or the other is an age-old quandary that has riddled humans from the beginning of time. Often it is the case that one of the two is keeping you from eternal happiness, and we don't have to say out loud which one we are leaning toward.

But what should be done in this situation? We've all been there. You are invited by someone special who has invited you to be whisked away for the week-long vacation of a lifetime to their two full bath timeshare in beautiful Maui to take things to the next level in your fresh new relationship, but your neighbor can't cat-sit Mr. Pickles because he's away on a forest bath retreat with his YA writing group upstate and you're cat-sitting *his* cat, Bella Swan. You could put Mr. Pickles and Bella Swan in a kennel . . . or argue why should Mr. Pickles or Bella Swan have to be inconvenienced just because you may have finally found the right person and tell your potential human soulmate to hit the road, chump. Plus, this week you already promised Mr. Pickles you would do his quarterly taxes (from TikTok residuals).

Much has been written on this subject, but without an evaluation, it's hard to tell if you even have a problem or not. Try to answer the following questions honestly. Only then can we consider a proper solution, which could range from an intervention to a breakup or a juice fast or getting more cats.

1. 🐾 **You consider yourself**
   A. an open-minded, caring person with enough love to give to BOTH a cat and a person.
   B. in an unfulfilling abusive relationship with a cat that thinks he's out of your league.
   C. undeserving of a real, mutually loving relationship with this cat.
   D. in a pickle.

2. 🐾 **Others consider you**
   A. seldom.
   B. a people person.
   C. an animal lover.
   D. moody. Because of this cat.

3. 🐾 The last party you planned was
   A. a birthday party for a boyfriend or girlfriend.
   B. an adoption anniversary for a cat.
   C. a birthday party, with a cake and invitations, for your cat's girl-friend, Bella Swan.
   D. an unplanned intervention at your place, where friends and family confronted you regarding, as they put it, "Mr. Pickles controlling your life and conservatorship issues."

4. 🐾 What quality is most important to you in a girlfriend or boyfriend?
   A. Is a non-judgmental listener who likes to cuddle and fall asleep on you.
   B. Provides emotional support on air flights.
   C. Is housebroken and has the ability to think *inside* the box.
   D. All of the above.

5. 🐾 On your profile
   A. you lead by saying you are a cat person.
   B. you state you are already in a complicated relationship.
   C. you have a picture of Mr. Pickles as your profile photo.
   D. you have no idea what it says. It was created by Mr. Pickles without your input.

6. 🐾 You're getting ready to go on a date. You
   A. check your appearance in the mirror and make sure there is enough food in your cat's food bowl.
   B. try to track down Mr. Pickles to ask what he thinks of your appearance.
   C. look good, feel great, and can't wait for this evening out.
   D. cancel the date because Mr. Pickles is in a mood.

7. 🐾 **During the date**
   A. you discuss your children but it's not until you share photographs that your date realizes that you are referring to your cats.
   B. you text Mr. Pickles numerous times.
   C. tear up and have cheater's remorse when your date orders the seared tuna.
   D. can't help but wonder how Mr. Pickles and your date would get along and suggest a Zoom at the table to find out.

8. 🐾 **At the end of the evening your date asks if they could come up for a coffee.**
   A. There is no way this is going to happen. Your apartment smells like you have twelve cats.
   B. There is no way this is going to happen. Mr. Pickles is just not ready.
   C. There is no way this is going to happen. First I learn that this doctor, who moonlights as an underwear model, is a dog person and now a coffee person? I'm a tea person.
   D. This is not going to work. To dissuade them, when they lean in for a kiss you cough up a furball.

9. 🐾 **For you, the third date means it's time to . . .**
   A. break things off.
   B. meet Mr. Pickles.
   C. pack birth control and a Benadryl.
   D. get the cat carrier and pack up some cat food and cat toys— Mr. Pickles is going on a sleepover!

10. 🐾 Studies show that over 40% of people would choose their cat over their partner. Let's say you are running out of your burning house. Inside is your spouse and Mr. Pickles. You can only run in and save one, for reasons that make no sense except for the sake of this quiz. What is your thinking?

A. "Wait. 40% of people would dump their spouse for a cat? This country IS crazy."

B. "Wait. Only 40% of people would dump their spouse for a cat? I thought that number would be higher. There's your Big Lie."

C. "Wow. It's finally here. That moment we all dread. My personal Sophie's Choice. I consider both an important part of me. I've been married three years and it's been the happiest time of my life. But I've known Mr. Pickles longer—he was there for me through all those years alone, through all those bad dates. Woo, this is a tough one. I find myself frozen in indecision. How did Sophie do it? That movie was like a zillion years ago and, it's funny, now I really don't remember how it ended. It doesn't look good for either of them and the time to have acted and run back in would have been like twenty minutes ago."

ANSWERS: There are no right or wrong answers. Like the cats we love, we are non-judgmental listeners, here for you to cuddle with.

"And where do you see yourself in 5 minutes?"

NAMES FOR CATS FROM ACTUAL FARMS AND NOT BARS

Butter Bean	Hay Fever	Roadside
Collards	Haystack	Ronald
Cupola	Jimmy Dean	Silo
Dell	Mr. McGinnis	Squealer
Fannie	Old Major	Sweet Pea
Free Range	Pitchfork	
Funny Farm	Purdue	

NAMES FOR OUTDOOR CATS

One cannot have an outside cat running around with an inside cat's name. It's not fair to you and it's certainly not fair to the cat. Many times, all involved are not sure if you have an inside or outside cat. Hiring a vet or cat expert is not necessary; this book provides you with a simple chart to determine your kitty's natural environment.

	INSIDE CAT	OUTSIDE CAT
PLAY TOY	Ball of yarn	Chipmunk
HOW IT ANNOYS PARENTS	Scratched furniture	Extended disappearances
DOWNSIDE	Total boredom	Rainstorms and bees
PERKS	Hero worship	High octave adventures
FAVORITE PRANK	Hid in house and made family go into a panic	Climbed a tree and made fire department show up

Animal	Columbus	Nature Boy
Baby Lion	Cowboy	Polar Bear
Bear	Grizzly	Scout
Bigfoot	Gunner	Squirrel
Boots	Killer	Tiger
Calamity Jane	Leo	Wild Bill
Catfish	Lion	Wild Thing
Cheetah Rivera	Marco Polo	Wyatt Earp
Coconuts	Moose	

PAIRS OF CATS

A wise man once said, the only thing more satisfying and joyous than owning a cat, is owning two cats. Two cats allow each to have a companion and someone to play with. It makes it easier to shop for cat food at price clubs, although I'm not sure why that would be. And it's easier in divorce court. If you give your two cats unrelated surnames, you are passing on an opportunity to show how clever you truly are (assuming you don't explain that you got the names from a book helping you name your cats).

Beauty & Beast	Hairy & Tonto	Pride & Prejudice
Bert & Ernie	Han Solo &	Simon & Garfield
Bob & Ray	Chewbacca	Sonny & Cher
Bonnie & Clyde	Holmes & Watson	Spongebob & Patrick
Captain & Tennille	Mulder & Scully	Thelma & Louise
Chip & Dale	Peanut Butter & Jelly	Tom & Jerry
Ebony & Ivory	Penn & Teller	Will & Grace

RESCUE AND RESCUERS

AlCATraz

Annie Bond, Vaga

 Bond

Aurora

Baby Jessica

Briar Rose

Captain Kitty

Cat Woman

Catalyst

Chivalry

Cinderella

Cindy Dewy

Clara Barton

Clarissa

Clem

 Kadiddlehopper

Damsel

Demoiselle

EMS

Emma Peel

Fiona

Flâneur

Freedom

Fuji

Gypsy

Hobo

Houdini

Iron Cat

Katniss

Kimmy Schmidt

Lost N. Found

Lucky

Oliver

Patty Hearst

Pawshank

Persephone

Ragamuffin

Ransom

Rapunzel

Refugee

Savior

Shawshank

Stray Cat

Support Cat

Sweet Polly

 Purebreed

Urchin

Vagabond

Vixen

Waif

Xena

Zelda

CHURCH CATS

There is nothing cuter than a church cat with a church cat name. Whether you received your new cat from a church or perhaps you plan to start taking your new cat to church when it's old enough, here are some names sure to catch everyone's attention on Sunday.

9 Lives	Charlie Chaplain	Holy Mackerel
Amazing Gracie	Church Cat	Meow Magdalene
Angel	Galilee	Pope
Bishop Boo Boo	Her Holiness	Saint Snuggles
CAThedral	Holy Cat	Sister Snookums

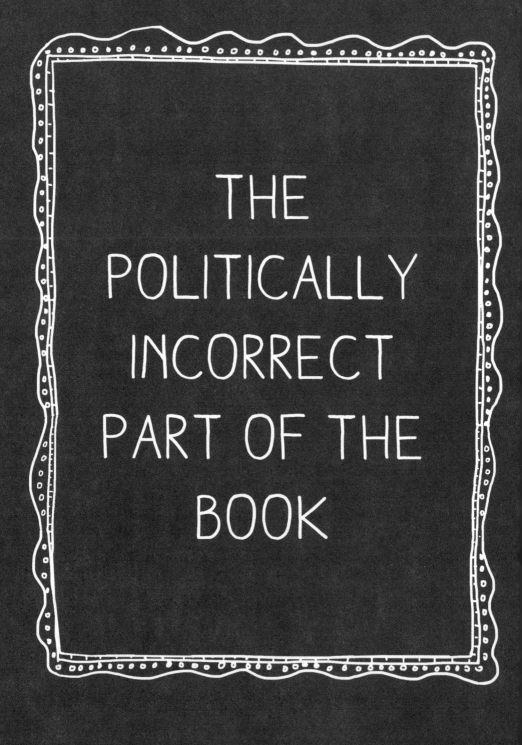

THE
POLITICALLY
INCORRECT
PART OF THE
BOOK

THE FOLLOWING ARE PARTS THAT GOT CUT

from the book, rightfully, for various reasons. But, I'll be damned if they didn't make their way back in!

NEUTERED CATS

Bachelor	James Spayed	Sterile
CATstrate	Mr. Fixed	Zip-Zip
High-Pitched Eric	Pocket Change	

I AM NOT A CAT

It wasn't that long ago that a lawyer pleaded he was not a cat when a picture of a cat appeared on Zoom where he was supposed be. But there are actually real cats who also think they are not cats. You've seen them. They think they're dogs. We say, own it. Have a dog's name and confuse everyone. Heck, go one step further and, every so often, change your cat's name. It's your cat. Do what you want.

"I blame the cats."

Boomer	Puppy Cat	Spots
Bubba	Rex	Stetson
Buster	Rover	Woof
Mack	The Situation	
Max	Snoopy	

WHAT *NOT* TO NAME YOUR CAT

This list is self-explanatory—make sure you avoid these names for your cat. It is only going to make things bad for you and your cat down the road. No need to invest time on this list unless you happen to be naming an enemy's cat.

Barf-field

Calamity James

Cat Lady Gaga

Cat Scratch Fever

Cat-astrophe

Claritin

Couch Potato

Cyclops

Dandruff

Elvis Cat

Feces

Fluffy

Hairypants

Home Wrecker

Lucifur

Mr. Hair Ball

Meow Tse Tong

Money Pit

Mousellini

Nicotine Patches

Psycho Cat

Puke Skywalker

Puss N Suits

Putrid

Road Kill

Stink Bomb

Sudafed

Three Eyes

Tuna Breath

GOOD NAMES FOR POSSESSED CATS

Fluffy	Phantom	Warlock
Morticia	Ravenclaw	Zombie

SCOTTISH CAT NAMES

So few Scottish cats have Scottish names and that's a shame, because there are some excellent selections to choose from besides "Haggis."

Arthur Kitten Doyle	Nessie
Ginger	Plaid
Kilts	Pudding
Lulu	St. Andrew
McSorley's	Scotch Whiskey
Macbeth	Sean Connery
MacCuddles	Sir Walter Cat
MacPedigree	Tabby Burns
Mary, Queen of Cats	Tatties
Moggy	

JEWISH CAT NAMES

Mazel Tov, on your new cat! Whether you decide to raise your cat religious or not, you'll want to leave that option open by giving your new cat a proper kosher name. This is best done before your cat is circumcised.

Babka

Bubble

Chatzpah

Furklempt

Kibbler on the Roof

Kosher Kat

Kugel

Latke

Lester Fluffstein

Mr. Kvetch

Mayim Bia-Lick

Mensch

Meowskovitz

Meshuggeneh

Oy

Purr Mitzvah

Purr-strami

Tchotchke

Verklempt

TRAILER PARK CATS

Billy Bobcat

Cat Lady Gaga

Catcall

Hairball

Nicotine Patches

Road Kill

JAMES BOND VILLAIN CATS

Your cat will be forever grateful to you if you come up with a name for him or her from a James Bond movie. The only name that would make your cat happier would be Food. Cat Food.

Barron von
  Snagglepuss
Blofeld
Bond, Vaga Bond
Boris
Catapult
Cat-astrophe
CATraband

Claws
Contessa
Curiosity
Cutie Patootie
Dr. No on the Sofa
Fluffy
Foxy Feline
Gold Paws

Golden-Eye
Jinx
Knuckles
Octopussy
Pussy Galore
Ruffian
Thunderball

CUSTOMERS WHO BOUGHT THIS ALSO BOUGHT;

EYE PATCH

GLOBE

INDUSTRIAL LASER

ADULT KITTENS: PORN NAMES FOR CATS

Communal Kitty

Deep Coat

Feline Groovy

Felix the Bad Cat

Fluffer

Fluffer Nutter

Free Fur-all

Friskies

Ginger Cougar

Kinky Boots

Kit 'n' Kabooty

Kitty Kitty Bang
 Bang

Misty Stray

Tom Cat

CATS THAT REFUSE TO USE THE LITTER BOX

Granted, not every cat experience is a fun one. And it's times like those when an owner needs to maintain their sense of humor no matter how difficult it might be. For cats who perceive the litter box as being too small, more like the size of a postage stamp, we present you with this list.

Mr. Headache

Messy

Missy

Mops

Poop Fairy

Scat Cat

Squirt

Stains

Surprises

Tinkle

U Kitten Me

IF ALL
ELSE
FAILS

OKAY, THERE IS ONE *MORE* LAST-DITCH

effort before we fully refund you the cost of this book. First find a quiet sun-lit room that is maintaining the ideal temperature for name-deciding (72°F, 22°C). Place two chairs in the center of the room with your kitty sitting opposite you. We want you now to stare into your cat's eyes while reading off this list and see if any of these get a reaction. The slightest twitch or blink may have to do. If you spot ANY reaction, you've got a winner.

Abbey

Abominable Snow
 Kitty

Adso

Affectionate Mew

Alias

Alsatia

Angy

Annette Fullajello

Ashley

Asian

Aspen

Babe

Baby

Bacon

Bad Kitty

Bambino

Basik

Bealfire (from a
 character in *Once
 Upon a Time*)

Bean Bag

Beari

Beezus

Ben ("short for Benrock
 Buckthorn" —Geoff
 Augustine)

Big Kitty & Baby Cat
 (Con Chapman)

Bimota

Bo

Boddington

Bogo

BooBoo

Bosco

BowTie

Bridey

Bruce! ("after
 Springsteen" —Peter
 Chianca)

Buddy

Burr

Caspian

Catfriend

Caty McCat Face

Catzilla

Cecil

Celia

Chai, Mao Feng,
 Oolong ("named after
 teas" —David J. Loehr)

Charlene

Cher Khan

Chidiock ("after
 Chidiock Tichborne,
 the 16th-century poet"
 —Elizabeth Wolnski
 Smoki)

Chloe Ruth
 Rosenbaum

Chunk and Mikey
 (from *The Goonies*)

Cielo

Claudius-Kevin

Cleopatra

Coco

Conte Biancamano

Crackers

Crash

Cray Kray

Creature

D.J. ("short for Duchess
 Junior")

Dante

Day-Z Mike

Dinah

Dirty Girty ("she had a
 lot of kittens")

Doreen

Dulcie

Duncan

Eartha Kitt

Edward McBean

Eeno-Nino-Cherry

Elpinoe

Ernie

Esme

Ethel May Potter

Fezzick

Fiona

Flint (grey tabby)

Fluffy

Frankie

Fusge

General Scipio Africanus

Ghost ("after a wolf in *Game of Thrones*" — Ashley Lotz)

Gillie (short for Gilgamesh)

Gizmo

The Good King Snugglewumos

Grace

Gus

Guzzi

Hammie (from the comic strip "Baby Blues")

Harriet

Henry of Monmouth

Her Royal Heinie

Hissyfit

Hypothetical Cat

Ignatz Mouse

Imperator Publius Aelius Hadrianus

Inky

Inky ("short for Enkidu")

Jack Mittens

Jane

JoJo

Jupiter

Kalani (short for Liliuokalani, last queen of Hawaii)

Kanye West Franchi, Dr. Jill Bader-Ginsburg, and Miglino Franchi Biden (Jamie MIglino Franchi)

Karma

Kasha Varnishkas Rubin

Kiki

Kirby

Krazy Cat

Kryptonite

Lady Elaine Fairchilde

Lambchop ("after the Shari Lewis: she would capture a mouse and place it in the bathtub, where it could not escape" —Kathy Kuhl)

L.C. ("short for Little Crash" —Martha Miele)

Lenny

Lestat ("from *Interview with the Vampire*" — Kosmic Kat)

Lilith

Lilliput

Lily Marlene

Little Mama

Little Phil

Little Rock

Lola ("who prances like a showgirl" —Jane Honchell)

Lucy Van Pelt ("because her head was large proportionally and she was bossy")

Luna

Mr. Sneezy

M.O.C. ("short for Mean Old Cat")

Magellan

Masha

Matilde

Maverick

Max

Medjet

Meghan Markle

Melky

Mercatoe

Mercury

Merlin

Michigan or Michy

Mika

Mikko

Minna

Miss Kitty

Molly ("with a Y, she hates Mollie with an IE" —Amy Ferris)

Mon Choy

Montana

Moofie

Mookie

Moonshadow

Mootsie

Morgan

Motown

Muriel

Nando T. Kitty (tuxedo)

Neo

Nimbus

Ofoeti

Omar

Otis

Pemberton ("after the street in Philadelphia; her sister, Elfreth, for Elfreth's Alley, and Puffy for a favorite book, *Puffy the Puppy*" —Janden Richards)

Peppy

Pepys

Phoebe

Phorever

Phrannie

Phreddie

Piewacket

Pilchard

Pip

Pipples

Pocahantus

Poe

Pogo

Poohette ("cross between Winnie the Pooh and Smurfette" —Christine Medley)

Pooky

Princess Kate
  Piddleton, aka Piddles
Professor Fluffy
  Bottoms
Ramona
Ramses and Tut
  (brothers)
Raul
Razor
Renfield
Rocco
Roger
Ron
Roomba
Roper ("named after
  the stove brand" —
  Esther K. Smith)
Rum Tum
Seger
Shakespeare

Shante
Sharon
Sierra ("because he
  loves high perches")
Sir Andrew Auecheck
Sir Toby Belch
Smudge
Snoop
Soot
Special Patrol Group
  ("from *The Young Ones*;
  one cat but she's the
  size of a whole group"
  —Nina Bellisio)
Squeaker Leo
Steph Purrrry
Sydney
Sylvia's Mother
T.V.
Talkie

Tavia
Theodore don Gottos,
  Jr.
Tristan
Triumvir Marcus
  Antonius
Tuck
Tuesday
Tyler
Vienna
Wanda
Watson
Wince
Winchester
Woodstock
Woody & Jake
Zelda
Zoe

NAMES THAT HAVE NEVER EVER BEEN USED BEFORE

You managed somehow to make it all the way through the book to this point. And you still have no idea what to name your cat. Here is a last-ditch effort to help, a short list of names that were erroneously previously left out of the book.

Adorable

Billy

Catwoman

Greta

Hooray

Huddy

Lester Snooze

Miggy

Millie

Mr. Scruffs

Poison Ivy

Shmpoouchy

Snooze Button

Will

Willy

Yarnball

Zook

ANSWERS TO THE WORD SEARCH ON PAGE 52:

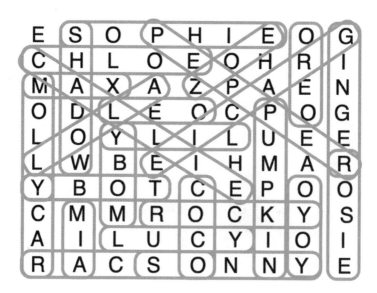

AFTERWORD

IT'S BEEN OFTEN SUGGESTED TO ME THAT I

was a cat in a former life. On the subject of reincarnation, coming back as a cat or dog is a far more common premonition than the idea of coming back as, say, a butterfly, tortoise, or whatever. With this planted in my mind, I often find myself staring into the eyes of a cat and wondering if that kitty was once a friend or neighbor or perhaps someone famous, like Liberace or Barbara Stanwyck.

I don't think that about dogs, and I have a rock-solid theory why. 1) If people came back as dogs, dogs would never poop in public. Let's say you're a beagle now. Wouldn't you be a little self-conscious? Plus watching your owner pick it up in a bag . . . don't dogs wonder why they're saving it? 2) If dogs were once people, wouldn't they want to watch people get undressed? Dogs don't care when humans are naked or do stuff with each other. If you dress in front of them, they couldn't care less. What's up with that? And finally, 3) (and this is the clincher): If you came back as a dog, would you ever lap up dog food the way dogs do? Game. Set. Match.

Now cats on the other hand . . . people certainly were once cats in their former lives. I have proof my nephew was once a cat. The kid sleeps until noon. When he moves about, he is already thinking about a nap. When he naps, he likes spots where the sun is coming in from the window. He is very finicky about food, but when he does eat, he licks his hands. He's studying computers in college, but I swear this is due to his fascination with lasers. His favorite activity? Laser tag (and *Call of Duty*). My nephew has ruined furniture by jumping on it and once threw up on my rug. He is skittish to any loud noises like vacuums or screaming. He has knocked over a family heirloom before. He hates baths. I've put warm bowls and milk with cookies outside his room and he always finishes them. Finally, my nephew is moody. One minute he wants your attention and acts out (e.g., smashing the car, putting food in his ears), and other times he needs his space and is standoff-ish.

So, all your suspicions were right. Cats might actually be someone you knew or will know later in life. That cat may one day be your boss in another life—if your cat isn't the boss of you now—so treat them well.

This one last part may seem weird, but if you should find yourself suspecting you own a cat that is someone from a past life, or maybe the other way around, you meet someone you think was a cat in a previous life, then one possible response is to conduct a séance with these people (or cats). It would certainly help with coming up with a good name and maybe answer questions haunting you late at night. No need to make it a big fuss. Just a standard séance. Maybe also reach out to the most famous cats in history at that time. There have not been many. Most were animated. Most live cats are not very animated.

FAMOUS CATS

The Cat in the Hat

Choupette (Lagerfeld)

Felix

Fluffy

Garfield

Grumpy Cat

Hello Kitty

Mr. Bigglesworth

Mr. Jinx

Morris (the Cat)

Socks (Clinton)

Sylvester

Toonces (the Driving Cat)

Speaking of Toonces, many years ago *Saturday Night Live* got a lot of mileage (pun intended) out of the car-driving cat (which was written by Jack Handey). Now that people are traveling more, there has never been a bigger calling for cats to drive automobiles. Yet there is still no written driving test for cats. Until now.

The following test would be administered for felines obtaining the new Class Y driver's license.

1. 🐾 The safest speed to drive your car:

   A. Is the posted speed limit.
   B. Depends on the weather and road conditions.
   C. Depends if your paws can reach the pedals.

2. 🐾 As you enter an intersection with four-way stop signs, you see a car to your left.
   A. You climb onto the sunny windowsill of the testing room and stay there for the rest of the exam. Your day is over.
   B. You meander to the front of the room and rub against the leg of the test proctor, purring.
   C. You proceed through the intersection since you have the right of way.

3. 🐾 The car behind you begins to pass you. You should
   A. meow.
   B. maintain your speed so traffic will flow smoothly.
   C. slow down slightly then hiss.
   D. floor it.
   E. sit on the horn.

4.  Assuming that the street is level, what should you do after you have finished parallel parking in a space between two other cars?

   A. Pee outside your litter box.

   B. Scratch and destroy the car's rich Corinthian leather.

   C. Pounce on the gas pedal.

   D. Sit on the horn.

5. If a truck or bus in front of you is making a wide right turn where you also need to make a right turn, you should:

   A. Quickly turn before the truck or bus is able to.

   B. Squeeze between the truck or bus and the curb and find yourself stuck until the fire department comes to your rescue.

   C. Play with a big ball of yarn for hours.

6. You are driving in the middle lane of a three-lane expressway. A car begins to pass you on the right, but the driver flashes a red laser on the road.

   A. Immediately jump from the vehicle to chase it.

   B. Swerve into the other car, forcing it off the road, then leap out the window to chase the laser.

   C. If that wasn't enough, you freak out because you misread the Car Wash sign you passed for Cat Wash.

7. Now you're riding a motorcycle. Do you wear a helmet when motoring at night?

   A. No, because you think you would look silly.

   B. No, because you may have to cough up a furball.

   C. No, because the helmet squishes your little kitten ears.

   D. Why should you? The child riding in your sidecar is not wearing one.

8.  The primary cause of automobile collisions is

    A. chickens crossing the road.

    B. curiosity.

    C. laser pointers.

    D. dogs using their cell phones while driving.

    E. other drivers going into shock when they see a cat driving an RV.

9. To operate a tractor you must have at least

    A. a Class CDL license.

    B. a cute matching reflective safety vest and collar.

    C. a pretty big yard.

    D. Really? You have me driving a tractor now?

    E. all of the above.

10. You are driving a commercial vehicle containing tanks of gas down a 25-degree decline. You should . . .

    A. avoid any sudden turns.

    B. take a nap in the sleeper berth.

    C. downshift immediately, if you can reach the stick shift.

    D. Use your cat-like ability to calculate the perceived braking distance from the next vehicle and sit on the horn.

    E. lose focus due to an empty cardboard box.

11. You are approaching a railroad crossing when you hear the sound of a can opener.

    A. It could be tuna.

    B. It has to be tuna, right?

ACKNOWLEDGMENTS

CAT LOVERS ARE A SPECIAL GROUP AND I'M

indebted to their participation and passion for felines. Thank you to everyone here who helped with this thoroughly enjoyable book, sharing the names of their cats. I hope they are pleased with the way this book came out. NOTE: This is the thank-you page and not more suggestions for your cat's names, but if one of these catches your fancy, I can connect you with the contributor and ask if you could use their legal name.

Cathy Widmark

Charlotte & John Kuczynski

Adrienne Sioux Koopersmith

Michelle Nachtrieb

Carol Brooks

Blair Thornley

Carolyn Waddell

Jessicat Fletcher

Claire Minges

Kathleen Krach

Joe Wos

David J. Loehr

Jen Robinson

Mitch Kaplan

Dawn Mockler

Jim Howerton

Phyllis Zickmund

Claire Beck

Becky Lindow

Beth Koehler

David & Melinda Stone

Katherine Pushkar

Pamela Ramenda

Diane Letulle

Paul Nesja

Cathy Honey

Frank Michael Angelo

Katherine Anne
  Stebbins

Teresa Ryther
  Pashoukos

Richard G. Marcil

Emily Pascal

Amy Rogers

Wendy Cook

John & Marlene
  Donnelly

Arnold Zwicky

Nina Bellisio

Beth Lawler

Melanie Rosenbaum

Ericka McIntyre

Leslie Ulrey

Valerie Uram

Jill Werts

Katherine Thornberry

Susanne Hohne Koster

Margo Smart

Lisa Solod

Diana Blomgren

Patty Jane Hoffman

Rick Parker

Michael Maslin

Justine Bylo

Jessica Delfino

Melanie Siegel Rubin

Richard Rosen

Jack Handey

Lauren Forsch

Gil Menendez

Jay Sacher

Chris Davey

Liana Finck

Kurt Opprecht

Diana Ani Stokely

Robin Sneed

Stephen Cole

Rob St. Amant

Pam Cario

Deborah Guarino

Erin McParland

Amy Rogers

Jennifer Clements

Colleen O'Neill

Phil Johnson

Dawn Mockler

Lisa Levy

Drema Dial

Darlene Coetzee

Gary Justis

David Kurie

Ellen Usery

MaryAnn Kapacs

Paul Kelba

Sandra Miller

Jeff Hobbs

Jos Wos

Tom Tanner

Amy Ferris

Mark Stamaty

Keith Knight

Ed Brodsky

Susan Mitchell

Nick Spooner

Stephanie Rose

Diana Blomgren

Peter Barberie

Alex Sinclair

Carol White

Elizabeth Ahlers

Alison McKenna

Andy Schulkind

Ian Boothby

Karen Green

Mike Sacks

Xeth Feinberg

Danielle Deschenes

Meryl Sklut Lettire

. . . and to everyone who suggested a cat name to me throughout my lifetime: thank you for being in the book.

And special thanks to my editor Ann Treistman, art director Allison Chi, the team at W. W. Norton, and my personal team here: my mom, my wife, and Joy Tutela.

ABOUT THE AUTHOR

Bob Eckstein is an award-winning *NY Times* bestselling author, illustrator, cartoonist, and world's leading snowman expert. His home in Pennsylvania is like a zoo.